THE HEADLESS MAN

A Novel in Prose Poems

OTHER BOOKS BY PETER DUBE

Beginning with the Mirror: Ten Stories about Love, Desire, and Moving Between Worlds (Lethe Press, 2014)
Conjure: A Book of Spells (Rebel Satori Press, 2013)
The City's Gates (Cormorant Books, 2012)
Best Gay Stories 2012 (editor; Lethe Press, 2012)
Subtle Bodies: A Fantasia on Voice, History and Rene Crevel (Lethe Press, 2012)
Best Gay Stories 2011 (editor; Lethe Press, 2011)
Madder Love: Queer Men and the Precincts of Surrealism (editor; Rebel Satori Press, 2008)
At the Bottom of the Sky (DC Books, 2007)
Hovering World (DC Books, 2002)

THE HEADLESS MAN

A Novel in Prose Poems

Peter Dubé

An imprint of Anvil Press

Copyright © 2020 by Peter Dubé

All rights reserved. No part of this book may be reproduced by any means without the prior written permission of the publisher, with the exception of brief passages in reviews. Any request for photocopying or any other reprographic copying of any part of this book must be directed in writing to ACCESS: The Canadian Copyright Licensing Agency, One Yonge Street, Suite 800, Toronto, Ontario, Canada M5E 1E5.

"a feed dog book" for Anvil Press

Anvil Press Publishers Inc.
P.O. Box 3008, Station Terminal
Vancouver, BC V6B 3X5
www.anvilpress.com

Imprint editor: Stuart Ross
Cover design: Rayola.com
Interior design & typesetting: Stuart Ross
Author photo by Paul Litherland
feed dog logo: Catrina Longmuir

Library and Archives Canada Cataloguing in Publication

Title: The headless man / Peter Dubé.
Names: Dubé, Peter, 1962- author.
Description: Poems.
Identifiers: Canadiana 20200185535 | ISBN 9781772141559 (softcover)
Classification: LCC PS8557.U23243 H43 2020 | DDC C811/.6—dc23

Printed and bound in Canada

Represented in Canada by Publishers Group Canada
Distributed in Canada by Raincoast Books; in the U.S. by Small Press Distribution (SPD)

The publisher gratefully acknowledges the financial assistance of the Canada Council for the Arts, the Canada Book Fund, and the Province of British Columbia through the B.C. Arts Council and the Book Publishing Tax Credit.

For Mathieu with Love

"I am the headless daimon with my sight in my feet; I am the mighty one who possesses the immortal fire; I am the truth who hates the fact that unjust deeds are done in the world; I am the one who makes the lightning flash and the thunder roll;

I am the one whose sweat falls upon the earth as rain so that it can inseminate it; I am the one whose mouth burns completely; I am the one who begets and destroys; I am the Favour of the Aion; my name is a heart encircled by a serpent; come forth and follow."

from *The Greek Magical Papyri*

Contents

The Birth of the Headless Man / 9

The Headless Man Sees / 10

The Headless Man Hears / 11

The Headless Man Feels the Sun for the First Time / 12

The Headless Man Dreams for the First Time / 13

The Dream Answers the Flesh / 15

How the Headless Man Found the City / 16

The Nipples Tighten / 18

The Headless Man Enters Town / 19

The Headless Man and the Bridge / 20

The Headless Man Gets Lost / 22

The Voice of a Lost Staple / 23

The Headless Man Climbs a Tree / 24

A Woman on a Cellphone / 25

The Headless Man Discovers the Crowd / 26

The Street Preacher's Voice / 27

The Headless Man Takes a Chance / 28

The Headless Man Goes to the Bank / 30

The Headless Man in the Public Square / 32

The Headless Man and the Law / 34

The Headless Man Understands the Crowd / 35

The Headless Man Remains Silent / 37

The Headless Man Riots / 39

The Headless Man Cries Without Knowing Why / 41

The Headless Man Goes to the Movies / 43

The Luminous Screen Goes Out / 45

The Headless Man Feels Wind on Rooftops / 46

The Headless Man Finds the Border / 48

The Headless Man and the Neon Lights / 49

An Animal Skull's Voice / 50

The Headless Man Dreams Again / 51
The Headless Man and the Volcano / 53
The Headless Man Discovers Music / 55
The Headless Man and the Stripper / 57
The Headless Man Knows His Hand / 59
A Hand Finds the Headless Man / 60
The Headless Man Thinks Out Loud / 61
The Headless Man Starts a Fire / 63
The Man in a Uniform Speaks / 65
The Headless Man Understands What It Means to Be Headless / 66
The Headless Man Contemplates the Tomb / 68
The Headless Man Knows Birdsong / 69
The Headless Man Takes His Desire for Reality / 71
The Food Truck Man's Voice / 73
The Headless Man in Love / 74
The Headless Man Meets the Vanishing People / 75
The Headless Man Goes to the Leather Bar / 77
The Headless Man Gets Head / 80
The Headless Man's Revelation / 82
The Headless Man Meets the Storm / 84
The Reflecting Bridge / 86
The Headless Man Gives Head / 87
Erection / 88
The Paper Boat's Account / 89
The Headless Man at the Threshold / 90
The Headless Man Reaches the City's Limits and Burns / 91
Acknowledgements / 94

The Birth of the Headless Man

When the noise of his birth subsided, the Headless Man woke to life. And so our tale begins with a lie. The truth is, at this point it would not be entirely fair to name him headless; his head lay at his side, eyes blinking into wakefulness with him. Still, he did stir; he found his feet and stretched his arms above him, past the point where his head should have rested, were he a natural thing. But he is not.

Rearranging all the images of his intrauterine fantasia, he stretches again, discounting the blank spaces around him. On the river, slight silver boats sail against the wind and the birds sit and sing around him, happy because something is about to happen. And it does.

The Headless Man takes up his head. He knows the day is about to begin and he is eager to be on with it. With the fingers of his free hand, he closes his eyelids. He hides his head among the roots of the tree, in whose tangle his first memories are trapped, tumbling.

The Headless Man Sees

Being headless, the Man had returned his head to nature for a time; after all, he is equally without eyes. Coming to this awareness, and realizing the power of his curiosity, the Headless Man finds this a problem.

He sits on a rock overlooking the road to the city and wonders. There is something out there, he knows. Something marvellous. Something that can change him. Something that will unlock locks, sting, make him cry, shatter silence, transform metals into artifacts, sow fields, tell stories, both spread plagues and heal them, help strangers, hurt friends, do the reverse, climb tall things, sing, learn, undo. Something that matters. And something that matters to him.

Yearning, the Headless Man reaches out for the empty space before him. Spreads his fingers. Flexes them. He wants what is in the world and wants the world alike. Then, because in the marriage of touch and longing, things reveal themselves to us, the Headless Man begins to see.

The Headless Man Hears

For a long while the Headless Man stays where he is, in silence. Not a sound rises from him, nor does any sound disturb him. Everything is timeless, unpunctuated, free of texture. Without any points of comparison, it takes time for him to understand that such continuity is a kind of incompleteness. What is not responded to, what is undisturbed, has no content.

Holding his fingers to the sky, he measures the passage of the sun across its expanse. Fingers fluttering, he watches the moon change shape. But having no ears, he does not count these things as rhythm. The Headless Man waves at the world. Sun. Moon. Sun. And moon again. Over and over. Time passes unmeasured for him and yet he knows there is more to all this than image. More than the delight and dazzle, the dimness and the fading out of form. The vanishing outlines of bodies in mist and twilight. The patterns marked out by the expansion of the trees' shadows as the day wears on. The V of flying birds. The spray of water throwing itself at land.

And then something stirs in his entrails, a movement that shakes his flesh and skin. Had he a word for it, he might call it "rumble." The Headless Man is hungry, and his body speaks to him. Fill me, it says. Move me anon. Give me something to wrestle with. The sound inside him is limited thunder, the hiss of the tide. Mountains turning over in their sleep. His belly makes sound to match the movement of the world. And the Headless Man, deep in his guts, begins to hear. This is noise, he thinks. This is the beginning of knowledge.

The Headless Man Feels the Sun for the First Time

Knowing the dark, the Headless Man recognizes difference. In his tripes he hears thousands of boulders slide from the mouths of caves; clouds part above seas so motionless they reflect the great invisibles whom the Headless Man knows are his familiars; his hands rise in the thrill of the moment. Seizure. Vision. Resolution. Spending. The lion-guarded gates of seventeen separate vanished cities shut for the delight of opening again. The man who sees through fingertips feels a great yellow sentiment take root. Take him bodily. Usurp his sense of what he is. And how. And where. His pineal gland, buried under a tree at the centre of his sensual evidence, grows erect. Leaving behind him every image he has come to love, he grows more attentive; he knows the source of images yet to come. Every fibre of his skin shivers in a tangible light, imagines waves of pleasure capable of razing categories—waits in noise on the amorous twilight.

The Headless Man Dreams for the First Time

Sensible, the Headless Man grows tired. Though the road ahead of him tempts, he lies down in the tall grass to consider. To consider the passage of time, the sound of air moving through vegetation, the possibilities for things to articulate themselves. He crosses his arms on his chest and knows why he cannot close the eyes he does not have. He makes a fist.

Sounds fade. So does light. The pasture strokes his newborn skin and calls up sighs. As he rests, the Headless Man feels the earth rotate beneath him; feels the activity, the constant, relentless unfolding of change. Beneath his back is vegetation, growing from rich dark earth, among which mill the legions of insects, worms, incomprehensible single-celled varieties of life. Swarming and swirling, teeming over and, more importantly, under everything. Feeding and feeling and fucking. Endlessly busy. More riotous than the currents of the air, more meaningful than we imagine. The Headless Man feels the long stalks of greensward fold over him and knot. Knows the creeping things move up them, across him, and begin to spin. They spin slender filaments of silk that cling to him, cling to the plants and the stones. Across legs. Across belly. Across breast and shoulders and arms. Over the remnants of his neck, they spin and bind until he can no longer move. Still, they spin and bind. Until muscles struggle to flex and fail.

The Headless Man is motionless, bound. Exposed to air and light. The army of the creeping takes him, swarms across his body chittering. Some utter, in voices so slight they pass all but unheard, faint and single vowels. Others, a single digit, one simple number. Each of the sounds is insignificant, but collectively they build. Grow loud. And louder. Overwhelm. Numbers and vowels ring in the rush of multiple legs. A howling. Until it stops and every living thing is silent. And the bound man struggles again. Struggles beneath the gathering clouds. And then.

The Headless Man sits up, startled awake. For a moment he does not recognize the space around him, or himself in it. Tall grass. Dim skies. But the road is still there, still stretches. The road is always open, always offers distance. This he recognizes first. This is enough.

The Dream Answers the Flesh

And lo, a man appears in the world: naked and headless. His cock hardens in the unaccustomed light and a wind rises. Stern, the moving air, moved, rushes over him.

The flesh of the face flenses off. Strips the visage bare, to bone. White bone, all chattering teeth. A blank. A descent. A sudden silence.

The shoulders go uncrowned. A slip, and where there were genitals, a skull—bone—smile: swallows a laugh.

In a bed a naked male body: tightens.

How the Headless Man Found the City

Because the trees were all but motionless. Because the sun was low. Because he was not bound. Because he was nimble; curious; undecided and unafraid. Because of the presence of colour. Because of the pressure of time. Because of hope. Because he rose from sleep. Because he found pleasure in the doing of it. Because of the burgeoning of languages. Because of speed. Because of the way a single turn is so often sufficient to taunt the nerves. Because, in the end, the road was there. Because the Headless Man knows this and wants to travel.

Because, from the high point on which he stands, everything touches. Because sky meets river meets forest and lawn, hillock and the roots of mountains. Because the wind is impatient in its grass; moreover, it touches leaves that through the theurgy of photosynthesis turn sunlight into ordinary life. Because, for the first time, the Headless Man sinks in the sense of expanse; space opens all around him. Because winged things can fly. Because they do. Because those who cannot fly run. Because the air rings with an absence synonymous with joy. Because all of this aimless pleasure happens, all the time. Because everything overflows.

Except the road, the Headless Man thinks. He recognizes its purposes: one goes one way or the other. He sees, at last, that a road is defined by its termini: it begins and ends and takes on meaning only in being exhausted. That is why it leads somewhere. At the far end of the road, the Headless Man sees something like a knot: it doesn't expand, but traps shape, traps colour and movement, traps noise. That is the town, he thinks. Overcome, he sees what choice is.

The Nipples Tighten

Two moons, as it were, peaks and craters both, but perverse; we rise in the cool of daystart: ready. The body's gravity holds us in tense pleasure: ready for the air, for joy. Or molecules: covalent bonds quivering: an unveiled wonder for a source.

In motion and motionless, we orbit the solar heart now spinning in this new archaic torso.

The Headless Man Enters Town

Like paper unfolding. Like the movement of water, clear under sunlight. Like unspooling thread. Like a fall from a great height. Like music. Like the growth of intimacy. Like a single line of silk waiting on its others as a spider lowers itself from one fork in a tree to the next. Like breezes. Like charm. The road passes beneath the Headless Man's feet and it signifies unheeded.

One foot before the other. Once again. He walks steadily, his pace brisk, following the knot in his memory unsure of his arrival time. Once again. Indifferent to it; only the momentum touches him. Once again. Only the passage. He is comfortable in this and understands that comfort.

Like the dissolution of ice. Like the climbing of flame. Like a sound that moves one and remains unrecognizable. Like the moment when two hopes meet and transform each other. Like sweetness. Like a belt tossed aside. Like wonder.

Then the knot in his memory ravels and he passes over the bridge.

The lights and the sounds await him. They are bright, even garish, and they engulf. They are potent and they support crowds. They rush. They stop, rush again. They overcome. They articulate. And they are not what he expected; the Headless Man knows anew.

The Headless Man and the Bridge

It spans space and that suffices, the Headless Man reflects. And still, it opens onto the void. The Headless Man comes to this bridge by following observed light: usurper of the continuity of sky. The bridge is clad in lights: bright, animated patterns that rise in space and then undo themselves in commemorative patterns. This drew him in; now walking at the limit of the span, the Headless Man remembers—or imagines he remembers—another view of emptiness: a cliff he wandered on, and there was a little dog too, the sharpness of whose voice responded to the wind. That encounter was unlike this; the dog—a witness—transforms everything. If it is real. Now, teetering at the verdigrised frontier, the wandering, acephalic viewer must imagine how he looks, the way this shadow reaches and recoils, expands and then returns to meet his nervous feet in the uneven luminescence that plays along the bridge. The Headless Man must reconceive his presence at the edge. Does the shadow grow forward to the past, or backwards, anticipating what is yet to come? The water flows below him, negating any questions about time. He sees five snails crawling on his chest, so slow as to be motionless, extending every moment of their lives and burdened by their domesticity. They vanish then. The water still moves on, and he, responding, reaches out. Pulled at, he shakes his absence of head; why throw himself down? This process, flow and reasoning and exultation, will go on, and he will remain, regardless of this choice. The Headless Man waves at the river as the lights go out, only to begin again.

The Headless Man Gets Lost

A bridge across the river. A shopping centre. A gate to a university. An entrance to another. A police station. The shadow of a broadcast tower. A window display of glass. The sound of an owl unexpected in the daylight. A subordinate clause misplaced. A mechanical dripping. The Headless Man. An abandoned staple. The memory of a rainbow. The smell of smoke on morning air. The future site of a bank tower. A coughing. A clock. An animal skull discovered on the back seat of an abandoned vehicle. A woman on a cellphone. The crying child one cannot see. The spoor of a wild animal long extinct. The promise of pleasure. The place where the Headless Man had rested. A blank in the memory. The lure ahead.

The Voice of a Lost Staple

A hastening man. Sans eyes. Sans mouth. Sans anything with which to measure time, he would make it after his fashion. Joining things with motion: lines of pleasure. A time for exultation, a momentary rush. Another one for or toward— not work, of course, but knowledge surely. Desire lines for the labour of the gut, the hand, the memory. The sex.

Manifold to a fault.

I too a silent refutation of those that sunder things. Abandoned by categorization, I join. Hold parts of the world the one against the other for the shuddering delight. For friction. Legible.

Sundry by default.

The Headless Man Climbs a Tree

He is walking, the Headless Man; he is searching. He traces with a measured pace the gridwork of the streets, the interstices of the lanes and alleys, squares and plazas, storefronts and double-dealing subway entrances that open up onto shops. Above him curtain walls go up revealing nothing: an empty stage for a performance—determined as a flow of traffic. It ends in accident and darkness coming down. Gripped by a perversity that unbends habit even as it soothes, the Headless Man seeks out a thing as foreign to the city as is he and yet as much at home. He searches for the place that most resembles him until he needs no more. Treading carefully, he is released from care by the apparition of a tiny park that takes him in: his vision and his body, takes him in. He is conjured by the single tree that rises at the centre of the formal lawns and flower beds: he replies.

The tree too out of place; the tree too caught up in the city's web of forces, seen and otherwise; the tree too standing, waiting, silent but living; the tree too a sign; the tree too an encounter with the world that begins in darkness and spreads out in eager light. And so the Headless Man grips one branch, then the next, and pulls himself up. Limb by limb, he moves toward the trembling crown and knows that, buried among the roots of a now-distant tree, his head sleeps and dreams of whistling in rain. The Headless Man extends his hand for fruit.

A Woman on a Cellphone

I mean it. No. No head. I am talking absolutely no head. Walking around in broad daylight; how does that make sense? Impossible. You can't live with no head. It's impossible.

No.

No, I don't mean no head like that.

Later.

The Headless Man Discovers the Crowd

At the corner, near a park, a child tosses a ball into the sky, lets it fall: the toy is a world, its surface replicating the oceans and the continents in perfect scale. An old woman watches birds and squirrels summon courage to approach the seeds in her extended hand. Two lovers entwine fingers as they walk. A man in middle age spreads out a jacket and sits down beneath a well-groomed tree. On the sidewalk just beyond the gate, a knot of youthful figures set up a table and stack pamphlets on it, ready to assault policy, to parse injustice, prepare—they radiate hope—to persuade. A red car pulls into an empty parking spot. A lawyer shouts into a mobile phone. A man in a blue uniform sets his face. A rush of people weighted down with bags ascend a staircase from a buried metro station. The Headless Man stops—stays motionless. A man in a dark hat points toward the sun. A boy laughs, sings the chorus to a momentarily popular song. A dog barks. A bird of prey—unexpected in the city centre, and yet there—screams shrilly at some opportunity. A woman in a clerical collar lowers her eyes. A handsome man, still young but not a youth, runs his fingertip along the edge of a dressing covering his new tattoo. A woman adjusts her spectacles. Another stops walking, looks around. She seems to find it, whatever it is. Someone drops a set of keys. A girl on a bicycle manoeuvres around a bus. The Headless Man stretches out his visionary fingers and is flooded.

The Street Preacher's Voice

And behold: because the pillars of the temple are overthrown, the flood of anger, the excess of quick spoken words, takes the land. Signs fill the sky and abominations walk the dark streets. Surely if the swans break their silence, the tides will hesitate. Lightning cracks the sky.

Why do your hands tense? Why release?

Lo: the knowledgeable cover themselves in arrogance and garments of great price and the wise close doors behind them and against the world. Children speak in tongues and the beasts of the field fall before sunrise. It has been written hitherto: if there be no judgment, the traffic signals shall hold forth in prophesy. Who among us will bear witness to the birth of horrors?

Why do you let fall your curiosity? Why fail to listen?

You who see without eyes, who hear without ears and speak without a tongue—eloquent body. Portal of nemesis. Daubs upon the wall. Heart of the storm, the human tempest. Solitary. Shewstone made flesh. If you touch us, the last things take on form. Shed all. Tumbling of walls and flowerings. Change.

Why do your fingers close on air and point to emptiness?

The Headless Man Takes a Chance

The Headless Man meets paradox; as he looks for the city's deep places, his ambulations, his constant back and forth, have led him to a blank space. He has come to the mouth of one of the city's boundless tunnels (for the fathomless spreads under every surface): they are dark mirrors of the roads now run. And here, a table—cloth-covered and obstinate—awaits. A stranger presides above it: tall in the naked sunshine, face filling with light that takes the brown of his eyes to hazel. A blink and they are amber. In the glare, a series of metal hemispheres gleam at the centre of the table: math. The Headless Man stops and observes. Behind his navel, a voice says, Feeling lucky, are you?

At the hands of the stranger with mutable eyes, the shining severed globes begin to stir. They circle and they slide; they trade places and return. They jump, they jitter and, in agitation, pause, then start again. A sounding: Make your choice and find the lucky ball, and they slide again; they do. A voice behind him says, It's just thimblerig. Its bearer walks away, but the Headless Man stands on, alone, unmoved. Instead of a retreat, he reaches out. He always does.

His hand follows the other man's; it traces as he sees. His palm above a handback seeking something else. The man's hand settles on a cup; he lifts it.

The Headless Man's comes down.

The ball is there: a glass eyeball gazes up to take in the vacancy where there should be a head. It is neither brown, nor hazel, nor is it amber. It is black and goes unfazed by any light. It chases sky—stares up and waits for something to emerge, to rise, to win in deeper ways than this. And in this it parts ways with its manipulator; he looks down.

The Headless Man cannot, will not, do the same. The partisan of the stochastic, he follows that one dark eye; he chooses not to lose his grip. He holds to empty air, its movement, its return.

The Headless Man Goes to the Bank

Cold and bright. Bright and cold. It is the semi-material character of the space that he notes first. The precision of angles: implacable, measured, keen, and the glare thrown back by the floors when they encounter such rays as do succeed in sidling, oblique, through the narrow windows flanking every door but the central. Everything is, he thinks, deliberate; there is neither happenstance nor abandon in this place. And though it seems all silence to those who enter, trade, and leave, to a man without a head the hall is filled with tumult. He hears the cacophony of commerce, the clang and clatter of money changing hands, the noiseless hum of boundless transaction making haste across the limitless networks of commerce, the cries and outrage of its consequences, the death rattles of the social, the bang, bang, bang of accumulation. The gush of the centripetal.

He makes his way to the counter only to learn that no one can hear him; he has no voice for them. In his coursing hands, his fluttering fingers palpating the air, the light, he sees the reason why. These people are all head: a great blank space, a void and cavern through which no water runs is at the centre of them. Pierced and hollow, their torsos are a conduit through which everything passes but to which nothing can hold.

He turns to exit, picking his way across the gold of the tiles on the floor, the gold of the ornamental rails, the gold of the tentative, the fugitive light, the gold of placeholders clutched in every palm, the gold of the memories that stand in for more. The gold of crowns, and tombs, and empty wine bottles.

The Headless Man in the Public Square

Leaving it behind. Letting go. Turning his back to what is known, to all the comforts of the familiar, the Headless Man exits the ground-floor space in which he's questioned himself and closes the door behind him. He has known questions, found them in the interstices of his day and his surroundings, where he knew they were waiting for him. All the questions tagged with his absent name, his not-quite-companionship. What are the limits of the knowable? Where is the end of days? How is it funny? How, precisely, does ontology recapitulate epistemology? Is any love unselfish? How does one distinguish sound from noise? He stood in the centre of an empty room and pondered these, and more besides. On the vaulted ceiling of that room, a room in which nothing changed but money going hand to hand, a mosaic design of the four seasons mocked its own representation as he did so. How can one ever exhaust the Baroque? The door closes smoothly, but the Headless Man knows that air and invisible things still make their way in and out. The sense of impenetrability is belied by the tumult of the street. Lights flash red and yellow and green; wires throb with current and with signals overhead and underfoot. The landscapes of a thousand different island retreats sail by on the sides of buses. On a fence here, a cat stares down on a flock of feeding pigeons, and just blocks from the stairs on which he stands, another cat strides with caution on a mission that would mean nothing to him if he tried to imagine it.

Across four lanes of traffic, the towering depiction of a model, skin golden, lips pink, feigns a contemplative gaze toward the heavens, perfect in its emptiness, satisfying in its provocations. By a food truck, two companions squabble over whether or not to have another coffee. On the back wall of a bus shelter, a luminous screen pours out the fluctuations of the world's markets while the young woman waiting for a coach shouts out an indecipherable pain, tears not quite welling in her eyes. The Headless Man tests the knob of the door he's just swung shut, once again weighing his options. The silence of his questions swaying in the balance against the rush of answers waiting in the world. Turn: no movement. Turn again.

The Headless Man and the Law

When a car crashed. When the glass shattered. When the lights flashed and a slow crawl—methodical though blind, a spread past ambition, lost to hope—of blood moved beyond the seemly boundaries of flesh. When the tears and the attendant howling troubled the night and broke all easy resolve. When the air itself flexed with static, under the heaving of invisible waves with sad pretensions to connectivity. When heads lowered and shoulders fell in resignation. When hope did much the same and resignation struggled. When lights came on in darkened windows. For the first time, the Headless Man met the law.

He met it at a crossroads. When a noisy, dangerous, high-speed chase came to a concussive halt at a wall. When he saw the law's tight men pull a bleeding boy from the once-vehicle, a young man who raised his hands and, crying out, said, "No." To which the law responded with a blow, a momentary silence, and electricity. Which leaves aside the time it stood with the young man at its representative feet awaiting—not assistance—reinforcements.

Leaving the Headless Man, hands by his side immobile, unseeing, to wonder, "When?"

The Headless Man Understands the Crowd

Swirling. "It's a strike!" Churning. "We know how!" Racing. "All together now!" Whirling! "Dialectics." "Suture." Turmoil. "Failure." "Structure." "Superstructure." "Fall." The language blitzes past him, overwhelms and then moves on. A chaos of clauses, cases, phrases, stops. A signifying cyclone lifting off with an indifferent violence. The Headless Man struggles to freeze a word, a phrase, in place. Moving through masses of people, he attempts to end the rush and fails. Instead he stops himself. Stands still and lets it circle him, then circles through it: a great fish in a sea of sound. He folds his arms across his chest, abandoning vision and yielding himself up to sound. Everywhere men and women hasten, shouting anger, bearing signs. They clamour and cry out, too full of fury and of hope to not do so. They shout, demanding: yell with vision. The Headless Man listens, listens more and listens harder; he tries to shape the phrases in his mind, attempts to knit the words together into sense. But they are too many to free of anchor, utterly chaotic. As unruled as the people howling them. They are a swarm of stinging things descending on a bear; a rockfall in a darkened canyon on another continent; a flood rising to sweep materiality from a ghost town where the crops have failed four times too often; a swarm of comets burning out in empty space; a war of the unknowing lost against an unnamed enemy. They flash; they burn; they threaten; they kill the silence that once might have been. The Headless

Man follows them and loses, and is lost. He listens still. Waiting on sense. It doesn't come; instead his stomach aches. Contracts and opens up again for something more than noise. This idiom is nothing but phonology. That cannot climb the towering orthographic walls that mark its space. He seizes every word he can and watches it dissolve, a salt, or sugar grown wet. Then he gives up his struggle, surrendering to ambient articulation; lets it pour through him. He lets the sentences, the slogans, the songs fill up his belly where the hearing waits. They fill him utterly. They satisfy past meaning. "Demand the impossible!" The Headless Man would smile if he could. "Utopia is not a place, it's a direction." The Headless Man will understand.

The Headless Man Remains Silent

The Headless Man pauses, then enters a crowd of bodies and is overtaken: made ready to consume by chattering heads. "Who are you?" one asks. "What are you?" inquires another. "Where do you come from?" "Why are you moving so quickly?" "What can you tell us?" "What do you know?" "Are there others like you?" "Why now?" "What brings you here?" "Have you ever broken a mirror?" "Can you talk?" "What is your favourite number?" "Do you have any friends?" "Where are they?" The Headless Man stands still before the onslaught. "Are you sleepwalking?" "How does it feel to be different?" "Can you sing?" "Where do you stand on the dialectic?" "Do you favour military intervention in the current crisis?" "What music moves you?" "How do you deal with anger?" "How can you live without a head?" "Why are your hands shaking?" "What is your name?" "How did you get that scar?" "Do you have an agenda here?" "Have you spoken to the police?" "Are you lost?" "Where are you going?" "What do you want?" "What is on your mind?" "What is your origin?" "Are you like us?" "Have you registered with the authorities?" The Headless Man's arms hang by his sides, taking the questions on sightlessly. "What worries you?" "What is unproductive labour?" "Does darkness frighten you?" "Have you known violence?" "Are you wounded?" "Do you drink?" "Are you hungry?" "Are you dangerous?" "What colour calms you when you feel unnerved?" "Do you read?" "Have you got something to teach?" "Have you come to warn us?" "Can you see us clearly?" "Do you understand?" "What do you do?" "Who do you stand with?"

The Headless Man stands silent; such language as he might offer them would fail to signify. The crowd cannot hear him and he cannot make a sign. The source, his source, of language tangled among roots sleeps: imagining speech.

"Why will you not answer us?"

The Headless Man Riots

First, it seems the water is on fire, as if some spagyric interaction has transformed the world in the turmoil now obtaining. But no, the Headless Man reviews: these are another form of change; blossom of fire afloat, incendiary Nymphaea sailing atop the overflowing gutters, evading the trampling feet, stampede, the shattered glass, the hue and cry, the burning cars that seeded them, the unleashed batons, the crying and the terrorizing joy that swirls and at the heart of which the Headless Man stands erect, reaching toward the mob: assessing.

This is the centre; the thought arises. One path—a narrow commercial street—is lined by boarded buildings: complexions different, bricks and stone, panels of some synthetic, but every feature identical: raw, wooden, blank, emptied of sense and function and of pity absenting. The rare exception some scrawled cypher, some elliptical vulgarity. Another road is already overcome with water. A flood unleashed by armed and armoured men when this, the crowd, first gathered.

The Headless Man is in a crowd again, and he attends to the uneven beating of its heart. Where the dead eyes sealed, the board mouths of architecture meet the devastation of the waters, occupied by shattered glass. There are other roads, he knows, smaller, more concealed, darker than the high streets; they will have to serve for egress. For beyond the water, behind the blinded homes and commerces, the armoured men still stand, beating a baton rhythm on their plexiglass barriers. And here in the crowd, the howling has just begun.

The Headless Man longs for a voice and waves. Calls out for fiery blossoms more livid yet. This is the heart, he thinks; his entrails spin and make a sound like thunder. It echoes, and is echoed, and replies.

The Headless Man Cries Without Knowing Why

It isn't pain, the Headless Man knows; pain requires no explanation and this calls out for more. It passes all that. It isn't realization: sudden or long in coming. There is no way that it obtains. This is not that, nor is it confusion, an incapacity or lapse in knowledge or comprehension. No. None of these. It is marked by violent motion, and cannot stop anywhere despite the absence of goal, the void of discourse and the blank space in between them. The Headless Man's hands are crossed across his abdomen, behind which entrails coil and twist, turn in upon themselves, and skirt by other organs going—seemingly—nowhere. A forest hung in shadows and crisscrossed by tracks that circle back. A labyrinth without a heart and overrun by monstrous pain. Horns in the corners. Shaking under every floor. The Headless Man cannot understand his flesh.

He huddles in the corner of a vacant lot. Bound on three sides and yet something else. Having neither eyes, nor mouth, nor tongue, the Headless Man recognizes the negations. And he shakes, rocking on his folded legs, he shudders and wants to moan but can't. A silence past understanding. A blackness, blankness, and a form that isn't one. No tears. Not sobbing. Not communicating. Not just these. His body shakes, moves without a lust for progress. No hope, no hopelessness. No shattered tooth. No sudden darkness takes the sky. No flaw in any angle. Not anything. No rotten meat. No cold meeting. No failed pregnancy. Not any. No lie told carelessly. No bitter kiss. No crisis and no error and no lock. No. Unspeaking saying No. No. No. A door slams. A child joins him. A door opens. No.

The Headless Man Goes to the Movies

He knows that he enters the darkness even as the darkness enters him; of this, the Headless Man is certain. A door shuts athwart dazzle, across sound. The temperature of a body climbs without notice. Anticipated and welcome. The Headless Man finds a seat and waits, observing the negotiations of light and the absence of light, curious about the method, the modalities by which this conjures meaning. The blackness parts at his curiosity and yields a limitless parade, oceans of grey and shattered hearts, all yielded to the violence of the wind: that colossal indifference to us. Architecture is toppled and in the toppling freed. Storm. The order and the honour of generations are waived and whirled. Everything is silver, silvered, compromised in visionary intensity, and yet the Headless Man knows this passes: passage being the nature of things. Fingers fluttering in the dark. Colour arises. Pewter turns to peach, to hues of pink. The gloom of ancestors to a crude but comfortable blue. Brown bleeds from charcoal, reds from the tones of ash. Pyres and furnaces rendering memory. Alone in the vast gloom and without eyes, he sees wonders. Bereft of ears, his guts resound with new musics, sounds that beggar belief. The Headless Man raises his hands and lowers his centre of gravity to embrace the unknown till now. In the newly coloured world it begins. Green. All of it green. Overpowering green and glitter. A city made of precious stones refuses to throw open its gates. Angry beasts that should not fly take wing. Heartlessness and ignorance flee from their homes; nomads and deserts haunt those rear-view mirrors. There's no place like it. The set of lens, the fruitless promise of the optical; shut down the four directions, thinks the Headless Man, abolish them. Open it all. There is more to the world than this. His hands and his stomach are joined. Sound and sense in contact once, for once. How he understands. The Headless Man knows a civilization in the hot pursuit of its best shadow. This is it. Letting the darkness out. He waits for the lights.

The Luminous Screen Goes Out

Flashing begins it. Where the promises of renewed youth, lighter taste, cut-price tickets, the gains and losses of a dozen indices once glowed, a globe of light goes green. Revolts. Falls back. Rekindles and does not. Then fades, leaving magic in its wake.

ABRACADABRA
ABRACADABR
ABRACADAB
ABRACADA
ABRACAD
ABRACA
ABRAC
ABRA
ABR
AB
A

Nothing. Then wind rises.

The Headless Man Feels Wind on Rooftops

The same place, but above. The same place, but raised on its own axis, its shared history. A tread that moves never forward, but exalts; this, thinks the Headless Man in the air that crowns him, makes a staircase. Having come to the city, the Headless Man must now embrace architecture and in so doing climbs those stairs that define the blank spaces in every edifice and—like all blank spaces—take one higher (or more inward). Rising up on pressing down. Climb. Rise on analogy: these cycles of colour: red, vermilion, alizarin, amaranth, cardinal, Venetian; marigold, gold, canary, lemon, yellow. There are more, though the walls surrounding him remain what they are; he rises to nothing, save a door, a broad space, open air but never empty. The top of the city spreads itself out, level, accommodating; no colour but the white-haunted blue overhead, the grey underfoot that sounds to the step. Stepping out, the Headless Man is struck; the wind runs over him as over everything. It comes in a rush, the wind voracious, the wind unbridled, libertine, filled with sense and touch. It comes to him, replete with innumerable contacts. The wind that caresses ladders in the laneways of cities, both this and the battalion of them across rivers, across seas, and trees that stand with no self-consciousness awaiting that arrival, and the light-inflected surfaces of water, and bicycle wheels, and empty bottles, traffic signals, sleeping cats, stones and shattered plates, and clouds, the pages of books on café tables—ruffling, and fires somewhere too, consuming with abandon, and handsome men and women, monuments to moments and history whose truth is all but incomprehensible, and toys, and momentary pleasures shared by intimates, and balconies that offer views he is still to discover, and shutters open, shutters closed. The wind, indiscriminate, that limns the world, traces him. Affirming touch, tracing out difference and so creating continuity. The omnipresence of the atmospheric body that astounds. That elevation that just comes, then hurries on: an absent affirmation affirming what is never gone. Unrestricted; headless too. To this the Headless Man spreads out his arms and wishes for a tongue.

The Headless Man Finds the Border

The sky lightens and the clouds disperse, racing toward a horizon defined by the movement of the invisible, the path of air. They sail overhead, indifferent to the life of the town, the hour, the observer, and the risk of change alike. The Headless Man intuits their dispassion even as he discovers his own. The dawn is coming on, will accompany him in the barest hours. So he returns to the park where he first learned to climb. A first upward reach.

He traces impalpable lines of power between shops and parking lots, hieroglyphic towers and blank lanes. He imagines the webwork in his wake: the flows of energy and stopped hope, all analogues of the progress of air, all rising signs. These he rides in a forward sense until his fingers bow by his side. Tense and unclench. The Headless Man crosses the road. Step and repeat and stumble. Stumble more. The gait fails; the gate waits.

The entrance to the park is barred. Across the once blank space between the limits of the wall, a black iron barrier is padlocked shut. The Headless Man reaches out; the portal does not respond. He grips bars between fingers and thinks to himself, nothing ever stops but the human. Everything else is turbulence.

To his left, a pair of young men clamber over the wall, their shirts in their hands and their bared torsos reflecting the oncoming violet. The Headless Man imagines following them. The gate trembles in his hand. Everything is turbulence.

The Headless Man and the Neon Lights

Turning a corner; something new appears. A long look, two paths split by churning traffic, laid out in lanes, hemmed in by facades, faceted ziggurats. That shine. Shimmer. Challenge darkness. The Headless Man—for the first time—hesitates. Finds pleasure in it. Uncertainty has a taste like limes. And all that colour. Walls of it and porticoes that give on more. Here is blue. There green. Processionals of lavender and puce. The Headless Man can feel his skin take on new hues: transforming. He longs then to speak cephalopodically, signalling desire murmuring magenta. The lights flashing on skin, for him; he imagines robots going pale save for their crimson, blazoned lips. Made up. Tumult of twilight and shimmering neon lights. Pink. Yellow. Aubergine, and then a momentary darkness fills the long road, the caesura between towers. Then the lights come back. Rolling dice. Icy blue. The curve of a naked woman seen from behind as—stutteringly—the caricature of her face spins toward the passersby. Lemon-toned, a blade descends into the outline of a nearly empty plate. A great blank eye blinks. Teal. And orange. And off-white. Then the clamouring shadows again. The Headless Man imagines his skin still scarlet. Feels a great heaving motion and knows it's laughter. Tumbling through the labyrinth of him.

An Animal Skull's Voice

Small—that's the key to timelessness. One must go unobserved. This leaves one to observe. The right place matters too, that is perspective. Oblique or direct. But one must occupy a place. A corner, a shelf, a doorway, the back seat of a vehicle now burnt out. Let things change around you and hold on.

And enjoy partiality. Give up on wholeness. No structure endures like this.

Even he rushing around with his head cut off knows this. It is his incompleteness that makes of him a myth. The desire for everything that's missing.

Smallness. Shimmer. Accretion. Passages. A thing rising from the water, or the shattering of earth. Wait.

The Headless Man Dreams Again

The city turned upside down surrounds, and the Headless Man walks through it. The sidewalks are in the sky, become the crowns of thousand-year-old trees gone absent. Above them must be, he thinks, the bowels of the city: storm drains and sewers, subway tunnels and the secretive nervous systems shepherding power and data and wealth. All of it sucking in light, rendering darkness. Descending, the windows of the towers reflect and distort images, twist them in the accumulated grime awaiting cleaning. And the tips of the construction are uneasy spindles; they shudder with the weight they must now maintain. The outlines of the buildings quiver too; the suggestion of pain, unease, discomfort, and of nerves before the transformation. The Headless Man's fingers twitch at it; he moves on. Seizing, touching, coming to terms at the terminal points. A city upside down around him. An overturned eon. An inverted infinity.

The polished concrete spans, the curtain walls of glass all gleam reaching downward, sinking deep into the elemental world. The Headless Man stops, regards, his arms extended, hands spread in recognition, and in the instant knows it is not the world that has changed, but him. Above him the sky is wet and he is underwater. The city's uprightness is untouchable, though its representations remain malleable. The thought shakes him; his is walking through an image: the reflection of a city in accumulated rain that somehow covers him. He cannot know whether he has shrunk or the city has yielded to a flood. He walks submerged. The creature of a puddle.

The thought jolts him awake. Pulls him upright in a rented room where, now, the light pouring through the blinds leaves stripes across his torso and his sheets. This unchanged; the light perfectly symmetrical, its regularity constant. Merciless. Reasonable. Brutal.

The Headless Man and the Volcano

It was a volcano once, the Headless Man has heard. His entrails flutter, ready for the hidden to emerge: word and cadence, trope and assonance. For this he has travelled, followed them—sound and sense—to arrive here: the summit of the hill, the pinnacle of all the discourse, and a park. For it is a park: a place for rest, for play. The slopes below are taken by the crowds in search of recreation, or of afternoons spent lost in sunlight. But here, at the top, the Headless Man is nearly on his own. He has the view as well, though it means nothing to him as he paces circles round a concrete pond he found waiting.

Neglected through the fading winter, the water in the pond is dark with decomposing leaves, leaving depth unknown, beyond the calculating mind that worries at the orbit paced. And paced again. The Headless Man describes a circle around the unattended pool and, holding out his hands, his fingers spread, seeks out a vision—imagining in silence a world underneath until it rises, conjured phantasm, a pyroclastic vision of the rising magma, broiling as it comes. He sees it on the crest, and past that to the buried place of origin; the raw material of the world churning under pressure, filled with heat. All savagery; all freedom; all restraint abandoned in its coming, its arising in the world. The Headless Man observes: the leaves, the pond become a cosmic violence, eddying. The swirls and currents of hot red that gyre even as they die, the sudden fiery rushes and the fostering bubbles that achieve the surface of the world only to break in sulphurous fumes and drive one from the edge. The little flames that leap while seeming to burn without fuel. The rush toward the lip, the falling back, the hissing at the fall. The joyous and indifferent menace as the magma jumps into the air. He sees it all, smells it in the air, and hears the muted sound of pressure as it grows. He knows.

He knows it comes in all its visionary furor because his hands reach out, his body calling for a world responsive to our flesh, and knows as well he cannot, despite this, succeed in grasping the apparition. And none of this diminishes the realness of the thing; it is a vision and a tale, and these are things, material, enduring, and as moving as a blow, a kiss, a lie, a flash of light, a calorie, a crime, a promise made and kept, a silence following on it all, a hand raised in greeting, a hand closed on what is rendered, what is due. The sound. The sense. The conflagration. Pacing impatiently.

The Headless Man Discovers Music

Three closed doors pose questions: two are a pair, the other keeps a distance but is equally dark. Featureless. Black. Composed. Of metal. Resolute. Despite. The Headless Man has recognized an infinitesimal hunger in these things: the tiniest throbbing. A back and forth that folds in on itself: a pulse. The doors rise and fall, answering to some pressure on the far side. They jump with curiosity.

"Why not stop?" The pair.

"Why stop?" The solitary entrance. The thing alone.

The Headless Man stammers between them. Staggers. Wants first to touch the lonely door, next the two; cannot—at first—bring himself to it. Though the reasons for his reticence are fugitive, hard to explain. An orbiting satellite in the sky projects its content into the distance, into the future. He looks up, seeking reasons. Then lays his hands in the blank space between the ingresses, the stops. Immediately he spreads his arms so wide that one of them rests on each of his objects: pair and solitude alike. And as he does so, his body presses to the wall, his fingers splay and want to curl; this he denies, but his fingertips deny nothing and try to see through walls. Embracing the structure, he feels a rhythm on the far side, a pulse: an on/off/on he imagines is eternal. The pattern feeds on itself: immortal cadence. Throb. He cannot know whether someone stands facing him, leans toward him on the other side. If people dance, what longing, but the sound reaches out. Insists. Seduces.

Convinces. Baffles. On. Off. On again. The Headless Man presses into it; embraces: substanceless. Wonders if this, like the night behind him, might be what love denotes. Presses against it.

Knowing nothing with any certainty, the Headless Man holds on to the building, the structure, and the rise and fall. Joining them. Together. He asks himself if there is a glory of sound underlying every undivided thing.

The Headless Man and the Stripper

Alone, seated, short of breath, curious, surprised to be here, leaning back, separating himself from his memories, calm for now, filled with expectation, the Headless Man wonders at the qualities of shadow, the baroque proliferation of the dimness. There are layers of it; these might fold. There are curtains; these might fall. Why, he thinks—though the gloaming moves over him—does he feel nothing? And he does.

He is as empty as the stage, low before him: empty as the mirrored surface of it. Neither flesh nor reflection crowds. The reflective tile too is dim in the intimate gloom. It too anticipatory in the closeness of the basement room, as saturated with the twilight. The Headless Man shifts in his place and the illumination returns.

A unique column of light takes the half-shadow at the centre of the stage and doubles in the mirrored tile on its surface. There can be no confidence about whether the thing rises or falls. It is simply empty in its ways—however briefly. Then the dancer pulls himself into its insistent presence. The Headless Man jerks at the sight of the muscled back. The pillar of light both traps and frees; every movement of the nearly naked figure is an articulate tension, as beautiful as it is overwhelming. As excruciating. One arm rises with slow sharpness and the other follows; the air parts at its muscular, keen edge; the incomplete spectator dreams of rainfall, drums, and sacrifice. The nearly naked man turns. Comes back and turns again. So close one feels the disturbance of the air. The arc of possibility; the slide into the body's roots.

He wonders why, again, why the passage of the dancer-generated breeze strikes his intimate flesh like violence when the gloom does not. Then the beautiful naked man moves forward, sucking up light and shadow alike, and the Headless Man shakes. He sweats, feeling it.

The Headless Man Knows His Hand

Because he had touched his face and let it go. Because he had, with his own index, shut his eyes against the light. And because he had no longing for the darkness countervailing. Because he reached for the heavens and failed. Because he had tried. Because he had abandoned without sorrow. He, headless and alone, holds out his hands and lets all of because fall, just tumble toward emptiness. Toward motion free of meaning, unhinged from justification, motivation, pallor, and the appetite for cause. Something underneath the surface of the river breeds ripples and yet stays invisible. The Headless Man clasps his hands, as if in observation. Something beneath him, underground, shakes, he feels it in his buttocks, in his joints. The Headless Man reaches down; finds curiosity; finds his own cock and shakes it in response, moves on; finds the ground, the tangle of vegetable life. And he would smile if he could.

With eager fingers, he runs palms over the world, feels breath, rotation, proliferation, an unanticipated threat. And in the knowing of contraries, he knows his hand as well.

A Hand Finds the Headless Man

Tensing and untensing, we grip air. First. Then earth through which fire moves someplace far away, making its way. Where. Sound fails us.

Moving through space, we define it through the absence of contact. First. Then when we touch, sweat rises to the surface of the man's skin in a sensible pattern. There. Comes a reflection.

Touching each other, we begin to name things. Tactile. Dactyl. Interrogatory. Knees in the grass, clasping thighs. The belly. The torso. The erectile nipples. An empty space. Where sense has fled our curious architecture. And there between the thighs, a thing we shall surely give too many names.

And which responds to none of them. Silent. And interrogatory.

We ask it questions and it answers with motion. Sliding between registers. As do we.

We do.

The Headless Man Thinks Out Loud

It could be a dirty window opening on an upper floor; the light once muted, now made bright. It could be a bird appearing in the sky, emerging from behind a treetop, the edge of a building. It could be something left ashore as the tide recedes, or a glyph painted in strokes as high as a man who startles on turning a corner, entering a gloomy lot. It could be the sound of music filtering into the public world, muffled but seductive, through a door ajar. Or the bark of a happy dog. A sudden rain.

All of it is meaningful, all of it for me. I love the unexpected, of the sudden unveiling, of the suddenly laid bare I am enthralled. Small things can stop me in my tracks, can make me come up short. I love the apparition in and of a brilliant gesture. And I love the motionless too.

Mirrors in dim rooms. The opaque surfaces of ponds on a day of utter calm. Bookshelves in a library under night. The face of someone deep in thought, and caught. Abandoned buildings. Unused carousels and sleeping birds. The photograph one stumbles over on a rainy day while it lies waiting near a shuttered restaurant, the rainy day a holiday for some. And this, the gathering clouds that lower, lower yet. The love one has for a child. An empty bus stop. Or a bicycle locked up.

And I am curious about this catalogue of mine. I wonder at myself, and my capacity to long. There is some pleasure in the recognition of my fondnesses, in the assembling of them. The shattering of silence matters here. The organizing of it by that care.

And still my speech is undetected. It is free—and though I am all observation in this, and mean no sentiment, because no one can hear me in the gathering storm, being without voice, I speak only from the heart and so go without hearing, absent understanding. I am beat.

The Headless Man Starts a Fire

Here are the words that rush to the Headless Man now: flame, kindle, incendiary, combust, ignite, lambency, illumination, heat.

They come unbidden, arise as he descends four slight steps to a black space in the city, a well before an iron-guarded window, where three men gather round a barrel filled with assembled trash—newspapers, government forms, circulars, more papers—and with wood freed from a neighbouring park, to trade their stories about the distant operations of blunt power that strides alone through night. The banks. The police. The houses of the parliament. The institutions of what's called higher learning. The dogs. And the batons. The crimson alarms on cars and the conspiracies. The men all have something to burn and a need for witness.

The light. The heat. The shine. The phosphorescence, incandescence, refulgency. The luridness. A glittering.

"It's up to you." The voice of an old man, head trembling as he speaks. A proffered book of matches in a shaking hand. And this the Headless Man takes up. And strikes: the fire bursts and leaps to life. Casts light on the wall and brilliance on the clustering men. Heads nod on those who have them. And all extend their hands. And murmur more.

The Headless Man knows he too will need to burn one day. The words come still: arson, char, scorch, singe, sear, incineration; and then smoke, cinders, grit, soot—and ashes. Ashes.

The voices round him fill.

Knowing this, the machinery of the social's limits, the Headless Man withdraws his hands; everything that burns must in the end burn out. Leave darkness all around. A trace.

The Man in a Uniform Speaks

Squaring the shoulders. Stiffening the spine. Tightening the muscles, his lips purse. One notes it. A word escapes: "No."

The left hand folds into a fist. The right reaches for something at the belt. A flash of teeth—white and feral as the tongue seeks them, sounding: "I said no."

Blue fabric turning black in the shade. Unexpected. Shade growing. Making space for light to show itself.

"No, always." Then the germ of affirmation.

The Headless Man Understands What It Means to Be Headless

Pressing hands against a mirror, the Headless Man perceives the trace of his passage through the world even as he makes it. On the surface of a doppelgänger creation fixed to the wall of a men's room, it lingers, his presence long enough for the fading to augment that ephemeral space. Watching: his feet shake against the tiles, and the language in his entrails turns over, chases the vanishing. The lexis slips into the gap between his body and the image of it. The hairs on his chest and legs stand up, erect, opening passage to the air as it stirs against his skin. His buttocks clench and elbows bend, pulling hands from the glass. Arms fold around his chest as the rise and fall accelerate. He embraces himself. A moment. In the glass it happens twice, slower at first. Faster then. The blank space between the rise and fall hides images of drying rivers, falling trees: of things growing, bearing fruit, and tumbling before lightning. An attic fire: smoke carrying forgotten keepsakes to the place where winds sleep. The Headless Man feels one knee eager to flex and show some reverence for the chaotic. And his shoulders rise. And his hands too, fingertips tracing paths from the imprints of his hand. Tributaries. A suggestion of the river that contours, holds, and then leaves behind the island on which stands the city—this city—he is learning. In the bed of that suggestion, past the silvered glass, an image he cannot see echoes his slumbering head where it conjures flowers and then fruiting. Where it waits. And suffers visions that make it bite its own lips, draw blood, lick it up again. Turning sensation into meaning. Its eyelids flutter but do not open; the Headless Man's arms release himself. Puts one hand back to the expansive, the profligate, glass as the other reaches for his penis, it too burgeoning.

The Headless Man Contemplates the Tomb

It is calm. And it is precipitated into the world from some someplace other than this, trailing angularity, anticipation, hard corners, whispering, and hope in its wake. Which wake closes on the trail behind it the moment it comes to rest. The stone and concrete know nothing of the gaze the Headless Man constrains. Nor his desire to reach out and touch the black facade: the thought of a silent leap, a ruby trapped in weeds, an unseen disaster. Clouds. Passages. He leans back against a naked angel carved and holding a trumpet that will never reach his lips; enjoys the clamorous silence and ignores the movement of the sun.

The Headless Man Knows Birdsong

Disputing with himself, he sets his hands free; coursing, they describe impossible worlds of both hope and fear; racing, they pull back from either; raging, they strike a sign whose centre is a knotted serpent pierced by a fluttering flag, and the Headless Man bleeds from his left hand; stanching the flow, his right presses against the open wound. And as it does, the bleeding man hears new sound in his guts. He understands the birds nesting in the tree, the birds passing overhead, the birds resting in the shadows of balconies and watching him with curious yellow eyes.

Here is what the birds say:

Low in a tree with bicycles locked to it, some nuthatches tell him, "If you will, eat your blood: understand it all."

"He should beware of all, for all can turn to betrayal," a pigeon murmurs.

"Yes," says a crow, "return to your head; feed it blood and cover it up well; bury it beneath rocks and mulch and hex signs. It will dream of wealth and lead you to it."

"He should go among sleeping people," says a fourth bird, on a wire. "Who understands birds understands dreams."

The Headless Man comprehends all this and acts accordingly. Holding his bleeding finger to an imaginary head, he envisions himself sucking up blood and sees in the distance, atop the hill at the centre of the park to the west, a great conflagration. The hilltop set ablaze and, somehow he knows, surrounded by a rampart of the sleeping.

He will go to it. He will follow the images in his blood. He wonders about armour. About beasts and blade and simultaneity.

The Headless Man Takes His Desire for Reality

The gutters are wet and the lawn soft; the Headless Man chooses to lie down among plants. Having known the city, he considers the horizon and contemplates the road; he thinks it never ends, begetting only more road; even the waters cannot stop it. Cities spawn bridges to extend distance. For the pleasure of it, bodies of all kinds move. Thus engaged, he chooses stillness: back against grass, hands in the loam transforming it. He lends it the shape of an old spell: conjures—calls up expanse, he too. Overhead the stars go on and on: prodigal.

In his joints, the Headless Man feels conflagration. Hips flex; shoulders fall back; his chest rises and falls as a vast, luminous havoc courses through his form. He loves it; he grows warm until, a long and shuddering breath its vehicle, the Headless Man lets the tumult go. Releases it into the world. In a form as imperceptible as it is extravagant, the mania rises—vaporous and resourceful. Fluctuating. One thing, then another, and always ludic. Taking flight and lapidary as it ascends, changing shape along that trajectory. The Headless Man names what rises: hope; knowledge; no—memory and thought.

Memory and thought spiral upward from his rising chest. They catch on a bending stem, a harlequin-blue flag, then slip off to tangle on a branch, a holly bough. They split for a moment, then come together once again and go on rising.

Thought and memory manoeuvre through the trees, are taken up by a rushing breeze, and climb still higher, spreading as they go: expanding in an upward spiral. Dip a wing as they cross the sightline of an upper-storey window across the street. They grow again and mount the moving air, their vaporous forms spreading arms toward the clouds awaiting them. A great bird, whose shadow falls across the Headless Man's recumbent body, casts a yellow gaze back at Thought and Memory. Then it precipitates toward some unknowable prey. He wonders if it hurtles toward the great carved bird presiding over the new knowledge he already sees in his future. The Headless Man longs to know birdsong once again, to give voice to that hurtling motion: that rush toward the world, the analogue of his own. To know it so as to recall it at his pleasure. In his mind's eye, he sees the world laid out below him as he spirals through thought and memory. From the heights, the grid of city is a page of graph paper on which the rooftops and the trees make patterns, pick out features. The peak of a nose. Pink gums studded with windows. Cheekbones thick with hydro wires. If his attention falls lower, his body lying here among them becomes the tight mouth of a metropolitan face. The lips ready to open, in laughter or in speech.

And he feels himself rushing upward. Falling toward the sun, following the trail carved through by thought and memory. He is breathless and still. Moving. Quickening. Anew.

The Food Truck Man's Voice

Soundless, of course: he has no head. No mouth. No tongue. But he points at the menu while the other hand cuts through the air, jittering with...nervous energy.

I imagine. Emphasis.

So, I make him his burrito. The same grill, the same ingredients, the same sizzle and vapours rising. The same pale green of guacamole, the same cheese, seasonings, and meat, the same motions, the same precision, the same wrapper, same everything. But nothing is the same; there's something new on the street, new in the world. And it's nonsense. Nonsense when I hand him the order too.

He receives it and it's gone.

The instant it is in his hand, the thing vanishes. This is nonsense too.

As is his silent turning away. His return to the street, the dimness between street lights without settling his bill. Who's to say he got his order anyway...?

Who's to say what there is to pay for?

The Headless Man in Love

He sits. He waits. He stands. He waits. He reaches out. He withdraws. He knows. Nothing is knowable. He waits. He looks inside: an ocean takes a step backwards, unveiling forms of life all but unimaginable. He waits. He looks toward the horizon. It flees. Then it draws near. He waits. He sighs. He waits. He calls out to a hundred familiar spirits. He waits. He dances in place. He sits again. He rises. Asteroids plummet through the blankness everywhere. He waits. The waiting, he knows, will end. He waits. The Headless Man knows at last: the waiting is good.

The Headless Man Meets the Vanishing People

It requires nothing but a corner, calls for nothing but the rounding of it. Nothing summons but the openness to new directions and a sense of ready space. The Headless Man has wandered into quarters of the town unknown, following the sounds of subdued conversation, lowered voices. Ephemeral discretion. Voices speaking words whose meanings escape the one still following them. The Headless Man turns away from the town's broad boulevards to find these three weird figures already in the gloomy side street he has stumbled upon. The trio trapped in conversation, hushed and thick.

They whisper to each other just beyond the radius of the street lamps; the Headless Man can feel the sounds they make untangle in his guts, where they effervesce without a sense. The tallest of them stands on towering heels and spins his arms with every syllable; hands and fingers tracing sigils in the air that put the Headless Man in mind of conferences, confessions, summonings, debate. He feels his own hands go up to offer a response; he pulls them back. The two accompanying the whisperer in heels seem dressed in gossamer; their shirts are sheer, and grey, letting the tattoos they cover remain visible in half light. They all lean in together, conspiring. The three heads turn at once, discerning him, and then tilt back.

In his entrails, soft sounds stolen from their exchange turn over and he hears the words "cock" and "eagle." Then "go"; it is always "go," the Headless Man thinks, and his attention slides to the side. Always go.

In the space of a single syllable, in the time it takes for the slight word to wind its way into his understanding, the Headless Man finds, on looking once again, the three weird figures are gone. They have vanished, leaving sequins on the pavement beneath his feet.

With hands outstretched, he sees a great, predatory bird on the horizon. Settling.

The Headless Man Goes to the Leather Bar

A first door: the Headless Man pauses. Above the door, a great dark bird—of wood and plaster—opens a metallic beak as if to tear at something, or begin a cry, or has just finished one. The thing's long wings spread above doors and windows, it broods over the place: a bird above what still waters, or what else, and what might hatch beneath such stewardship. The door is black. The windows on either side, as black, cast back dim reflections, suggest sinking, rising, something drowning. The place is named in black letters on black glass; the Headless Man—with memories of other doors ascending—speculates, lays his palm against the door and shoves. A second door across a tiny alcove: it hangs, a fall of rubber panels through which music finds a way. Behind which shadows move. The Headless Man goes on.

The room is close; narrow, just half as broad as it is long; a bar crosses the left end, and the man who stands half-naked behind it has little company. The room is sparsely occupied, eight or nine, but houses three more doors on its far side. The Headless Man goes on, his fingers taking in the images along the wall: of men, men bound, men nude, men covered in the hides of animals and borrowing ferocity in order to transform. Rough pleasures, violent joy, a weeping as the monsters sheltered in our dreams emerge; they transmute once again. Tall men, their bodies straining at the limitations, the frontiers of form. There's one whose eyes are shut. There's one whose mammoth erection constitutes a sign. An open mouth. A body frozen in its frenzy, as are all of these. Still men, these images. The Headless Man goes past them: one more door.

The sound of something cutting through air. The gleam of chains suspended from the rafters. A thud. A scream. A moment filled with tension halving, then proliferating. A man, his body crossed by thick black straps of leather punctuated by chrome, stands in a darkened patch, lips hesitating somewhere short of sneer. A tall fellow, long legs clad in chaps, has one foot up, pressing against a wooden crate from which the head of another young man protrudes, eyes banded against the darkness; light is fugitive here. In a corner two young men, one behind the other—who is bent at the waist—shine with sweat as the first, erect, pounds against his partner; the Headless Man sees visions of protoplasmic life, of cells pouring their substance into one another. The swamp, the source of everything. A man brings the sole of his boot down on the genitals of a muscled figure sprawled before him. Two men in the uniform of an imaginary legion, rigorously fitted and edged in red piping, kiss passionately as they gaze out at the watchers gathering around them. A man rests, reclining, ass exposed on a floating platform at the back of the room. He moans twice and men assemble round him, tugging at their flies. A young man kneels in a cage. A bearded behemoth pours beer down his throat. Flesh flowers here. Halving and proliferating once again.

There is a wound in the floor, a tear, an opening in which a wooden staircase descends to greater darkness. He circumnavigates it, passing a fellow who holds another's head against his groin, and greets him with a wink. The images outside this room were patterns, thinks the Headless Man. Or were not pictures at all but magic mirrors opening on a world remade for this. Not drawings but potentialities: horizons where light bends and falls apart in bands of colour. The whole room is, after all, bathed in crimson light. The men's bodies swallow it and pass beyond flesh, become stones, are scarlet jewels whose value defies calculating. Red lights transform everything: the sweat, the cum, even the sound is sharper. The sound that rises from the opening in the floor: a whistling, cracking rush that ends in a whack. And a whimper. The shadows grow hues, and cry as well. Multiplying.

The Headless Man feels hands upon him. Fingers on his chest that slide toward his nipples: stop. He asks what it might mean to have no head in here; he turns around. The door through which he entered is now gone. The wall smooth though covered with images. More mirrors double back the ceremonies of the space and offer no easy return. This other man pulls at him. Hands sliding toward his ass. "Let's go below," he hears in his guts. The Headless Man would smile if he could; no door to open here.

The Headless Man Gets Head

It starts in the hands. In the unfurling and clenching of the fingers as they close on another man's. The Headless Man knows—no, sees—it all. The fullness of the lips. The clatter of the nerves spitting images into the remote cerebral arena; there they mutate into timelessness. The amassing of treasures. The evocation of hungry spirits. The emptying of city squares. The tides. The southward flight of birds. The descent into darkness.

The stranger's hand held as they walk down the stairs into gathering gloom. Each step takes them deeper, and their contact grows. Mastering the staircase and avoiding the fall. Knowing the touch of a man. Returning it; the Headless Man at last finds an empty space. At the bottom of the stairs, a cubical midnight reaches out for them, takes them in its arms.

They move through a body of sound. The moans and moist susurrations of flesh stir together. The slippery hiss of sliding mouths. The odd slap shattering any recall of a pat world they'd embraced and in which desiring men are animated shadows.

They pass through a curtain of chains to enter a deep obscurity and head for its farthest point. Here the sounds are almost constant though more muffled. The flesh, erupting: the surge into proximity, the vanishing. The body glow unveiled and veiled again; the body glow erect in empty space.

The Headless Man and his partner find a deep place all their own, and their hands part, only for the other man's hand to find his acephalous partner's waist as he falls to his knees in perfect, impenetrable silence. The Headless Man would, if he could, gasp. Would, if he could, cry out as his body, beginning at the groin, stiffens and becomes all tension. Bone and cartilage, muscle and sinew, blood vessels, fluids, nerves, even the ceaseless, accelerating heartbeat become a kind of structure: a birdcage holding a brilliantly coloured fluttering impulse prisoner. Though temporarily. The winged thing batters at the limits of the body. Struggling. Yearning. Running riot.

Finding flight in the dark.

The Headless Man grabs the hands on his hips. Squeezes them. Moves then to his kneeling lover's head and rests them there, first riding the relentless back and forth and soon encouraging it (he cannot yet know this word). The darkness takes them both and everything else.

Until there is no need for hands any longer. No need for sound. In a blast of light so short-lived as to be all but imperceptible, the lover's mouth presses up against him; the lover rushes forward to see it. His arms go round the Headless Man, whose spine shoots skyward suddenly—and none of it endures. At the fulgurant moment the stars vanish; the other men too; the curtain of chain evaporates; the kneeling man diffuses and the Headless Man is gone. The body's cage dissolves, and the riotous fluttering bird, gone free at last, begins to sing.

The Headless Man's Revelation

Having gone down with the man who said "below." Having mastered the staircase and avoided the fall. Having known the touch of a man. Having returned it. The Headless Man at last can stop. A churning cloud of blackness falls, patternless. Here it opens, there shuts down, and opposite a crowd of flawless silhouettes rotates. Or doesn't. Exhausted in a darkened corner, holding a lover to his chest: wondering how this man might want to look him in the eyes. Joyous at the unachievable visionary dark and breathing deeply: sucking in the void and wanting to breathe it into the man with the unseen smile.

The memory of what was once the Headless Man begins to gather up the pieces of his abandoned form. He finds them in the tumult of the dark, in the cascades of the imperceivable. In memories. In grapes growing over-ripe on a slope in flames. A paving tile abandoned on the seashore. A snowdrift only starting to melt. The vase on a broad stone mantelpiece in a house on Guernsey teetering. A sleeping fox. The wheels on a skateboard overturned, spinning idly. A row of lights on some cinema wall slowly dimming. The back of a soprano caught up with her own reflection. Lumber: piles of it wet. Both sides of a coin somehow visible in the same moment—and both defaced. An image of his birth. A massive serpent, perhaps a python, uncoiling. The pattern of his hands in the air when he laughs. His footprint in a park, filled with insects determined to make their way out of it. A crack in the upper right-hand corner of one panel of tinted glass in a high wall. A sixteenth-century sextant lying on its side. His erection, subsiding in an ocean of blackness. A mass of shadows that overwhelm but for some reason do not threaten. A traffic sign with one letter struck out by an unnamed wag. The impenetrable obscurity of a basement left abandoned. The feel of his shoulders straining when he reaches overhead. The Headless Man in the animate murk observing. The black. The absence, all alone. The man's head against his chest; the knowledge that even this will end. A weeping woman in a river sobbing at the birdsong as she searches in its depths: those tears of joy that fill the current to flooding point.

A darkened hemisphere surrendering to the one in light. The change, and the Headless Man finding his feet.

The Headless Man Meets the Storm

It begins in the guts, like so much else. It stretches and turns, gathers strength, makes ready: the pressure, the swelling, uncomfortable but anticipatory. The Headless Man feels the coming sound, the fury at its warm-up laps. In the labyrinthine entrails at his core, a nervous feeling makes its way around the bends with caution; every turn is an admission, each twist a revelation. Something great and terrible is coming. The snaking corridors of bodily tissue are a test for understanding, welcome sound. Are processionals moving to the empty stomach in its place. And now the Headless Man rubs abdomen grown resonant as ozone takes the sky on its descent and crowds it to the breaking point; it opens in a tumult.

The viscera respond; he hears them as they trouble, as they leap to meet the squall that comes on in a wind filled with voices: a coloratura howls as a curtain falls, a sick child trembles with a gurgling cry, a cat calls out in heat, a caravan of armoured vehicles rattles by and loud on back roads whose ends remain unmapped. The storm responds, resurgent once again: the rushing air, a speech to an empty room, a squabble undertaken for the pleasure of perversity. Then thunder falls, a rage of angels: the Headless Man starts upright at the call, answering the blast that rings out in the space between his liver and his spleen. The fall of metals out of space. The last shout of a vanishing species. A great shaking in the clouds; an open space. And rain moves through the trees with percussive exclamations, here, here, here; it dampens walls and strikes the earth with all the hissing of the legendary serpent that circumscribes the world; that troubled sleep that breeds tsunami, swallows civilizations. A thought that drives the Headless Man to joy, to match the atmospheric rhythms with the stamping of his feet and more, to greet the tempest with the echo chamber of his still-beckoning stomach—eager, hospitable, longing—which he will fill with all this glory, all that noise. Sounds to carry with him always as he spirals, laughing.

The Reflecting Bridge

I love tension. Push and pull are an embrace every time: the dizzy pleasure of the interchange of terminals. Every end a beginning; every beginning an end.

The flow in two directions makes me happy. The agreement in opposition. Bow and lyre. Light and sequin. Come and go.

Centre everywhere. Circumference, none. Both walking a line and being one.

Your gaze strikes me and is returned, Headless Man. Doubled: one for each hand. Mobile for the joy in catching.

Communal at last.

The Headless Man Gives Head

The sky knits itself up above the tree beneath which the Headless Man's head still mutters in its sleep, telling stories of the drowning of worlds, the vanishing of clocks, the sunrise above deserts, and the odours of food. Mostly, however, it speaks of sensations that remain imagined to it, of movement: the swinging of arms, the touch of hand on skin, the tautening of erection, what it might be to run, to dance, to fall to the ground on sand or new-grown plants. To learn, to know. Interminable: the sky, the sleep, the stories alike. All caught in the gathering of clouds. Once slow, now quick, assembling overhead in a visual pleasure, a version at once; they close off the expanse of blue and menace, despite so much delight. Their portent is fulfilled as the sky breaks open in a rush that it falls—no, hurls itself—down. A rushing to meet earth.

The rain comes, violent. It bends grass, transforms earth, makes solids move. Shells, husks, and pebbles jump for dizzy company at last offered. Small living things scatter and claim what passes for higher ground. Rivulets take form, take life. Puddles are born. The ground throbs and the tree's roots sigh with wonder. And beneath those roots, within them, the Head's eyes flicker; cheeks flush; lips tremble and jaws grow slack as he recalls the dreams he has abandoned. The Headless Man's head opens his mouth and tastes water. Takes it in. Learns to love it, love the thirst that drives his eagerness and drives the world's too. Swallows everything. Returns it to the ground.

Erection

The hands, seeing pleasure in the world. Insist: response. My joy inevitable. The palms pass by and the future strips itself nude in the pattern of their criss-crossing lines; no one to read it. I am too far gone, am silence and anticipation. Between the straining legs but empathy.

Here, below a tree, this head in its autonomy lets out breath. Once. Again. A ragged rhythm then.

Deep in the skull, I am aroused: a stiffening. A pineal gland erect. A great light. A shout. A flooding at the roots. Glow flowing in the mire: me. A standing thing; a view above the rush.

The sky echoes with lightning. All but invisible, in the glare of day we meet.

The Paper Boat's Account

I was freed by a child, as from handlers, and left to find my way. Asail in the gutters that have become a world and the tracks of the stars, I rush forward seeking an impossible horizon I was promised. There: the vanishing point that gives the lie to all the mythologies of the urban.

Indifferent to the flesh of green apples brought here in airplanes; happy at the stains of wine tattooing my folded bow; laughing at memories of blue nights in dazzling snow. I recognize distance in the space between my vision and the collapse of structural integrity. Forward.

I am given my head for a time and find myself wondering about him, at the corner, who appears to have abandoned his. Where might he find himself? Or I. Run contemplated by electric moons, black hippocampi and microbes, hollow straws that swirl in my wake, passed by a man with a knife in his hand and a skull at his groin.

Soon I will tire of the islands of empty cans as I have of hands. I can only go on. Heedless. Fatigued. Knowing only that I must love turbulence and chop. And if I find, in the end, the maelstrom in a simple drain, let it swallow me up.

I will sail the underworld then, find through the cracks the cities in the roots of trees and love their citizens. There, wonders.

The Headless Man at the Threshold

Having pulled himself together, piece by piece, having left the darkness behind, the Headless Man confronts an eagle that alone stands between him and those fragments of the heavens that remain.

Roiling dark clouds rush in from the west, covering great swaths of the sky, but in between them some stars go on shining, burning away in the blank infinite. These the Headless Man's splayed fingers reach out toward from beneath the motionless bird of prey. Roughly hewn, crudely painted, and somehow still magnificent, it holds fast above him. Magnificent in its aspiration, magnificent in its artefactuality, it endures: a thing to gather under.

Then the rain comes back once more.

It comes all at once: fast, hard, sharp as blades, hissing like an angry, ancient reptile, striking every surface only to rebound into the air one last time, nostalgic for its source. And it gathers in rivulets before the Headless Man's broad feet. It falls in a blind fury—shows no inclination to retreat.

The Headless Man stays under the eagle's outspread wings—under its protection. He will not enter the rain right now. He doesn't want the wet, has no desire to wash anything away. No wish to be stripped of anything.

The Headless Man Reaches the City's Limits and Burns

Leaving the articulate darkness, he comes—at last—to the end of streets, the absence of architecture. By muddling down a slope, feet shuffling and knees nearly folding, he comes to the river and its endless indifference. The Headless Man, sated but eager, dizzy and uneasy. He knows the bridge flickers past his peripheral vision to the left, trading its gaud to the night for space, and he knows that, in his imagination, the mountain is aflame once more. But the sky overhead is cracking open. Gives a distant sound, a trembling; a flower erupts in the vault, the space of night, petals of colour uncreating themselves in wind, sparkle falling back to the world just left behind. Here a hyacinth unfolds fiery, glamorous as an unthinking youth, bright with the gorgeousness of a sun just past the solstice, settling. Wait. There an iris opens itself, opens itself again. Passing strangeness, and a fury in the sky. Cruel with untrammelled space, cold and far away, oppressive in its plentifulness, incomprehensible in the pointless splendour of its spending. Fountains of floral anguish—there, there, there, and gone, suddenly and forever, leaving an aching in the retina, a trace of colour, the smallest vestiges of light and finally nothing. And everywhere the human face absorbs its share of colour. The lips of a boy tainted with a bitter, citrus yellow. The arch of an ambitious cheekbone livid with the blue of noon. There, the Headless Man himself, stepping toward the self-renewing conflagration making its way out of the world and back, takes on his share of hue, wants to cry out. Pinwheels. Turning. The trails of coloured light are the lines of age on a sky that has seen too much, are untravelled highways in the heavens leading nowhere, coming back. Stop. It is a festival and the clouds have put on masks of sequins and dyed feathers, hiding their faces from the business of the world, and they are drunk with the blush of wine upon their cheeks, a smile where they wink. Once more a whistling high into the air and a flash of light, the wager of spring as flower upon flower blooms and perishes again. Rose, jasmine, and a honeysuckle hope—all collapse. Rise up and fall. The stillness of the air seems too alive. There is a sound of laughter. Stop. And in the river, everything repeats for pleasure, couples spectacular burns. And the Headless Man, knowing something he cannot speak, stoops, brings hands to the water's surface, and—fingers growing wet—sees his image burning too. His shape in flame, the place where the heart is bursting, conflagration, and knows it will not go out. Only change, and move on. Don't stop.

Acknowledgements

I owe several people, groups, and institutions real thanks for their support in the writing of this book. I will therefore avail myself of this opportunity to express my gratitude in a public way.

Among the earliest readers of these poems while they were in process were three people to whom I owe particular appreciation. I offer my deep gratitude to Jason Camlot, Andre Furlani, and Thomas Waugh; your insight, kindness, and guidance have been invaluable to me.

I must also thank the editors of *The Revelator*, Matthew Cheney and Eric Schaller, who published earlier versions of three poems from this book, David Nadeau who published earlier versions of two other poems in *Le Vertebre et Le Rossignol*, and Jason Abdelhadi and the whole editorial team at *Peculiar Mormyrid* who published an earlier version of "The Headless Man Dreams Again."

A very special thank-you is due to the one and only Stuart Ross, a remarkable poet, fiction writer, and the editor who oversaw this book as we shepherded it into print at his wonderful A Feed Dog Book imprint. I am delighted and honoured to join the impressive list of writers he has published over the years. His keen editorial sense and unwavering support of my work means a great deal to me. Thanks for being a real pal, Stuart!

Last, and far from least, thank you to Mathieu Beauséjour. My dearest friend, my partner, my great love story, and the best companion in life and art I could ever possibly imagine. This, like everything else, is for you.

Peter Dubé is the author, co-author, or editor of eleven books, including the novels *Hovering World* and *The City's Gates*, the short fiction collections *At the Bottom of the Sky* and *Beginning with the Mirror*, the novella *Subtle Bodies*, a finalist for the Shirley Jackson Award, and *Conjure: a Book of Spells*, a collection of prose poems that was shortlisted for the A. M. Klein Prize. In addition to his creative writing, Dubé writes on the visual arts and cultural issues; in this capacity, he is a member of the editorial committee of the magazine *Espace art actuel*.

Other Feed Dog Books from Anvil Press

"a feed dog book" is an imprint of Anvil Press edited by Stuart Ross and dedicated to contemporary poetry under the influence of surrealism. We are particularly interested in seeing such manuscripts from members of diverse and marginalized communities. Write Stuart at razovsky@gmail.com.

The Least You Can Do Is Be Magnificent: New & Selected Writings of Steve Venright, compiled and with an afterword by Alessandro Porco (2017)

I Heard Something, by Jaime Forsythe (2018)

On the Count of None, by Allison Chisholm (2018)

The Inflatable Life, by Mark Laba (2019)

Float and Scurry, by Heather Birrell (2019)

An imprint of Anvil Press